A Tribute To

CHRIST

LaShawnda Allen-Ruffin

A Tribute To
CHRIST

LaShawnda Allen-Ruffin

ISBN: 0-9787788-6-3

Printed in the United States of America

Published by:
Lumen-us Publications
4129 West Sauk Trail
Richton Park, IL 60471
Office: 708-679-1255
Fax: 708-679-1255
Email: Books@lumen-us.com
Website: www.Lumen-us.com

DEDICATION

This book is a tribute to Christ!

About the Author

LaShawnda Allen-Ruffin a Christian soldier for Christ has the desire and tenacity to win souls for the kingdom of God! She understands Romans 12:6 "We have different gifts, according to the grace given us."

Her delight comes from living her purpose and vision. She is a dedicated wife to her wonderful husband Ronald. She is the mother of two sons who are the rays of sunshine in her life, Ronald Jr. and Myles.

Lashawnda is a graduate from Illinois center for broadcasting. She is active in her community, and has a genuine care for the elderly. She has a zeal and zest for life, living her life's dreams and passion for broadcasting in television and radio. She is currently on air as a producer and announcer weekly in Illinois.

ACKNOWLEDGEMENTS

First and foremost I humbly give honor to the Master of the Universe. I thank God for awakening me to my purpose in life. I want the world to know all things are possible through Christ! It feels my heart with such joy to know God's mercy and grace brought this book into fruition. God has and will continue to supply my every need. I want the world to know God gave me every poem. He whispered to me every line. I take no credit for the work of the true author of the world. I will forever be humbled by my experience with him.

To Jesse White, Illinois Secretary of State and State Librarian I thank you from the bottom of my heart for being a tremendous support and well of knowledge. I appreciate you for allowing God to use you as a vessel to bring God's poetic instructions for life to the world!

In loving memory of Charard F. Henderson my sister, best friend, prayer partner and now my eternal angel.

Thank you, to the law offices of Vincent Aurrichio, 20 N. Wacker Drive Suite 2520, Chicago, Illinois 60606, phone 312-332-6410. Vince, your unwavering support and encouragement and efficient work ethics have been a pure godsend. Bless you and your practice and family.

To my family and friends, thank you for all life's lessons, they have proven invaluable. Thank you all for the gift of love through the fruits of the spirit, which is peace, joy, kindness, patience, and consistency.

Thank you to a phenomenal publisher, Marilyn Foster of Lumen-us Publications, for being the wind beneath my wings.

Thank you, Silver Enterprise Limousine, Inc. Chicago, IL 60629, phone 773-294-9083, for always providing superior service. "Making you feel like you are riding in the lap of luxury!"

CONTENTS

A Tribute to Christ!

CHRIST LIVES IN HEAVEN'S FLIGHT!

Christ lives in heavens flight!
From the early morning sunrise
when we first open our eyes,
to give our first fruits
should be our pursuit.

To love everyone we come in contact with,
to be a living example,
yes, that would be the perfect gift!

A tribute to Christ,
who endured cruel, unjust strife.
So that we may live and have eternal life,

In the golden gates of Heaven
where streets are paved of gold,
and laughter never ceases in the soul.

Where the spirit is free to fly,
and all your cares are no longer worries;
because on Him you truly rely.

And the soul shines bright,
from your eternal light
side by side with Christ the Lord on your personal flight.

What an extreme ecstasy,
God's everything you thought He'd be;
compassionate, caring, loving, trusting, and kind
no purer love will you ever find!

Transcend, but never take your eyes from Him,
stay focused on the light,
and enjoy Christ, in your Heaven's flight.

11

REFLECTIONS ON THE KING!

Sitting, reflecting on my circumstance
being mindful to give it just a glance,
"No worries," is now my motto.
Knowing my destiny outside is to achieve;

Soar beyond my most eminent dreams
why, because I reflect solely on the King.

King Jesus is so good to me!
He has the capacity to set you free.

Reflections in the annals of my mind,
thinking-prosperity, health, and wealth.
I surely will find.

Reflection on the King everyday,
outlines in my mind the way
the dreams and visions He has planned for you and me.
Goals He will bless us with to give victory!

SUFFICIENT GRACE

God is Omnipotent the Great I Am,
who will supply all your needs relentlessly;
because He can.

He's concerned, but wants you to learn
to rely on Him and Him alone.

He sits up high on His throne of grace
watching and willing to erase,
the pain and anguish you are going through,
with sufficient grace to pour over you.

JUST IN TIME

Lucifer thought he had me,
just in time Jesus grabbed me,
from the entanglement and the snares,
knocking back all fury and glares.

Just in time
Jesus stepped right in,
He reminded me,
we're closer than friends!

He's the Savior sent to this world
that we all may be saved men, women, boys, and girls.

Just in time,
He knows we all fall short of the glory of God,
He whispers "Repent!"
And mean it from your heart,
God will forgive you every time.
He will save, protect, and provide.

Just in time!

RESTLESS

Restless soul.
Out of control,
seeking the turmoil to cease,
constantly searching for peace.

Hands stretched outward,
afraid to look like a coward,
open your thoughts!
The price for your soul was already bought,
with the precious blood of God's son;

The only true one,
who can save your restless soul,
give you eternal peace to behold.

Move, reach, stretch, and grab for Christ,
this is guaranteed to save your life,
restless soul.

THANKFUL HEART

Thankful heart, at all times!
Thankful spirit, inner light shines!
Thankful soul, with all that's in me!

Cherishing Christ for all He's been to me.

A rock of refuge.
A friend to talk to.
A chamber that embraces all of me.

My confidant who never harbors envy,
the being that holds on to my mind,
calming, relaxing, soothing me to unwind.

To share, no matter what time day or night,
He's never too busy, or not there.
He's always willing to fight.

Yes, Fight for me!
No weapons formed against me shall prosper.
He said it in His word,
Which is the gospel.
This is why I have a thankful heart.

GOD'S JUSTICE

God's justice will cast away the wicked,
leaving all the righteous standing firm and divine,
all nations will come forth
to see His light shine.

OVERJOYED!

Overjoyed from the good news!
Never annoyed or confused,
don't let Satan knock you off your square.
Be assured God is always there.
Take comfort in believing,
His presence will help in relieving,

all the stress from the pitfalls of life
Christ has already made the ultimate sacrifice,
so believers can experience that after life.

Overjoyed!
Down deep within the soul,
a closer relationship with God can make you whole,
fill your existence thoroughly from head to toe;

Blessing you outwardly,
so others will know,
just who keeps providing you with all these miracles,
Tell them it's the King, the most high, the imperial!

 ## LIFE GOES ON

After your loved one is gone
memories fade from yesterdays
but never far away.

A familiar song
brings remembrance of happier times when,
times of smiles, touch, laugh or scent of your kin,
whether it was a loved one or a lifelong friend.
Life goes on,
for you it hasn't end
here on earth
believing God is a comforter for what it's worth.
The tears stream down
and your heart seems so full,
lean on God's unchanging hand
and remember the golden rule;

To live is just.
To die is gain.
Memories will ease the hurt and subside the pain.

Thinking quietly about life,
absence from the body is presence with Christ!

To close your eyes and still love in the mind,
helps the days seem easier you might find.

Leaning not to your own understanding
trusting God and His scripture
peace be still.
Love forever inside your heart,
being a Christian is the place to start.

To get on the path to victory
so that one day you may see,
your loved one or friend
waiting in peace for your eternal life to begin.

 ## COVENANT

The bond between me and the King.
It is uniquely intense
He's my everything!

It is the closest I have
the peace and joy makes me glad.
Grateful from the start of everyday
reliant and trusting He'll make away.

PEACE

Jehovah-Jireh!
My provider!
My constant peace,
The one I rely on to make troubles cease.

A friend like no other,
closer than a mother.

King of my peace
just confide in Him,
tranquility will increase.

Jehovah-Jireh.
In control!
Peacemaker for my soul
my slumber and my rest.

Peace for the spirit,
be still you will hear it,
like a calm after the storm,
He takes care of he who belongs;

Belongs to Him
like the implanted seed that will soon be a flower,
peace with the King will give you all power.

DREAMING

Dreaming of infinite possibilities
that God can manifest willingly.

Setting my sights on higher peaks
envisioning my transformation
before all kingdoms and nations.

Trusting in God's divine wisdom
to bless and mold me into fruition
dreaming one day of being an icon.

Spreading the gospel of Jesus
telling everyone who they can rely on
to give them all of their heart's desires
and their dreams
solely relies on the King.

Dreaming, wishing, praying, decreeing
having faith of a mustard seed
keeps you believing
God has granted your dreams.

MINISTERIAL LOVE

Non-conforming and true
stern yet confident to help pull you through,
ministerial love.

Ordained and in cue
to life's affairs and concerns

with scriptural verses to help you learn
your way through obstacles.
that seem to block you
from getting to the real you;

And weigh heavily in the turmoil of the mind,
the goals you have envisioned and designed,
reflecting as you rewind
over ways to be kind.

Loyalty, compassion, truth, companionship
in the end
to assist in
being your ministerial friend.

1:23

It's 1:23 in the morning
my body on the inside is turbulently storming.
My soul is weighted with despair,
praying and wishing you still care.

Down stricken with grief
feeling of bereavement just won't cease,
longing for what I can't have
praying for laughter, happiness and to be glad.
I know that I'm personally under attack.
The intensity is strong
I'm too weak to fight back.

I must give up

and pray to God to fight
hoping that He won't blow out my eternal light.

For all the errors I've made
the wrongs, I've done
down on my knees
before God's son.

My face filled with shame
praying my heart will unleash this terrible pain.
How do you not surrender to what you want and dream,
when boldly inside you're ready to scream.

Wait, I'm sorry, give me just one more chance,
I am a victim of my circumstance.
Help me God to run and flee,
your word promises you'd never leave me.

Sincerely,
1:23

DESIRES

Desires that are forged from premonition,
tantalize the soul when they come into fruition.

To love with all that's inside the heart,
gratifies the essence of three parts;
the mind, the body, and the soul,
open your life to behold.

What actually has been sent to you,
from Christ above,
realize it's not an accident it's love.

To love is good,
God equals good,
share your heart, body, and soul with all manhood.

EMOTIONS

Intertwined vibrations from the core of your soul,
indelible tensions intensely in control.

The complexity of the mind
seeking reassurance to find
the opening to allow the emotions to burst,
satisfying the emotional thirst.

Drinking freely from the opportunities
that cause your emotions to genuinely
give in to the power of love
knowing all good things come from above.

SWAY

Can I sway your spirit,
slowly and rhythmically so you can feel it?

Moving you gently from an upright position,
rocking or oscillating is my intention.

Sway,
to move you back and forth and pivot from the base,
veering and guiding you to that certain place.
Sway,
swaying you to be steadfast and strong.
Exercising influence and authority to keep you from wrong.

Recognizing your anointed, sovereign power,
thankful to God because you are His flower.

TROPHY!

We are the architectural ornaments
of the most high, omnipotent God,
representing a living victory
for as far as the eye can see.

Deep below the troposphere,
Satan is angry and filled with fear.
He comes after the anointed
but has no power,
because God watches us with love and affection,
surrounds us daily with a hedge of protection.

Even when we fall in public unrest
He promises to always give us His best.

Fight with the word—the love letter, the Bible,
remember to stand tall, and smile brightly;
knowing deep within, you are His trophy.

SWIFT RACE

The circle of life is a swift race,
express yourself
set the pace.

If you love someone, tell them;
Seize the day,
tomorrow may not come
and yesterday has drifted away.

Never have regrets, or ideas untapped,
follow the miracle inside, it's your heavenly map;
to unlock all the possibilities
life has in store,
Christ is the key, if you want and require more.

Be specific in your swift race,
have an attitude of gratitude,
it makes blessings move.

MIRACLES

Miracles going forth
in front of you to grasp,
the power is in the word of God,
you only need to ask.

Don't be dismayed about delay,
delay is not denial.
Oftentimes the test is in the trial.
Avoid the rapture at all cost,
be true to your light
so your miracles are not lost.

Know in your mind,
miracles come from Christ
and He's easy to find.

Consult your Bible,
a love letter from God,
so your journey to your miracle won't be hard.

Get your miracle!

LABOR

Know them that labor among you,
negative attitudes stifle the fruit in you,
be conscious who you allow to speak over your life,
expose the Devil's iniquities and strife.

Labor for healing.
Labor to be restored.
Break the yokes and reach for more.

Know them that labor among you,
have Christian armor bearers speaking positively, over you
and to you.

Labor for love.
Labor for power and conviction.
Labor knowing God's love holds no restrictions.

Labor to be heavenly bound.
Labor for your jeweled crown.

PASTOR

Pastor!
Shepherd of the flock,
directing, motivating, and providing keys to unlock
the rules and accolades of life.

Mentor, friend, and good shepherd,
teaching us what's right,
leaned on, pressed on, relied on, and constantly being used,
blessed and appointed for sharing the good news.

The leader, and the apostle, knowledgeable of the gospel,
the anchor, the ship,
praying you through it,
instructing you on your direct connect,

access to the best,
the most supreme God.

Preparing His church and flock,
not to have spot or wrinkle,
because He knows God will come in a twinkle.

Yes, in a twinkle of an eye!
The Savior will return,
Pastor is preparing you to not get burned.

ROSES AMONGST THORNS

Roses amongst thorns:
Mean people, angry people, violent people,
where are the nice people of the world?

They are there,
roses sprouting amongst thorns of despair,
relinquishing love at all cost,
radiating through
like a winter's frost.

Glistening with a hue,
that the thorns can't compare to,
sacrificial offerings of beautiful fragrance,
yes, that is there spirit;

Willing to show the inner beauty,
that matches the outer shell,
live your life to prevail,
elegantly wonderful;

Looking at the cup as half full,
operating out of compassion and love,
following the golden rule;
to be a rose amongst thorns.

 I WOULD LEAD!

I would lead,
destined to reign my pathways,
from high turning directions,
tells the cries found in desires.

Ancestry, history, legacy, and inheritance,
generational lifeline,
chase the dream, not the competition.

Define your pathway,
never conform,
just design and align your dreams to the Creator's master
plan,
always lead and stand.

HEALED

Looking beyond the images of broken dreams,
living beyond the obstacles and screams,
Healed!

To be healed from inner pains,
to aim for the stars in the sky,
never fearful of trying to fly,
Healed!

Soaring higher than your imagination,
with godly clout and expectations,
Healed!

Resonating in all wonders spiritually
that originates from the heavenlies
for all to see,
Healed!

Healed is your testimonial story,
Healing took you to glory,
Thank the Master we're healed!

BORN BLESSED

Are the words I express,
as I speak over my life that will manifest,
the dawning of superiority,
that delivers me from inferiority,

Born blessed,
shooting upward to a whole new level,
living by faith,
being steadfast and unmovable.

Astonishing the Devil,
who tries continuously to knock me off my square,
this can't be done, because Christ is always there.

Born blessed,
whether I 'm weak or strong,
to help me carry on,
to win the battle and the race,
Giving God the glory for His unwavering grace;

Because I am, and was...
Born blessed.

 ## GOD IS GOOD

Yes, God is good,
He's the great I Am,
giving us dominion over the sea and land,
granting us freedom to choose our own free will,
dwelling within our hearts,
saying, "Peace be still."

I am He who is, who was, and will be forever more,
from the highest heights to the ocean floor,
God is good, all the time,
His ear is in tuned to what's on our minds,

what's in our hearts on everyday,
Give God His glory,
Stop and pray.

Recognize, God is good!
He is the greatest from the north to the south,
the east to the west,
God watches us all at the same time,
because we are His best creation,
throughout all nations.

HAPPY SIDE OF LIFE!

To awaken with a smile
is the gift my child,
to love beyond misery in any capacity
is the happy side of life.

To detour from confusion and strife,
to set the example for another's life,
joyous years free from tears
is the happy side of life.

Knowing Christ is there,
when no one else cares,
to talk to, to lean on, to share the ideas you dream on
is the happy side of life.

To face each day and it's challenges,
to be confident in knowing who can handle it
is the happy side of life.

To figure it all out at an early age,
to love the prince of peace—
"Sweet Jesus"
is to be truly free from the cage;

The cage of life
that prevents you from having, attaining, and possessing
the happy side of life.

THE ROCK

The rock,
The shelter,
The foundation,
Provider for all nations,
Healer, a rose amongst thorns,
Giving the breath of life before you were born;
Loving from the rock.

FATHER

The earthly one
I never had,
you replaced that longing,
And Became My Dad.

Listening and encouraging me to go on,
giving me tenacity
not to quit and move on.

Understanding truly I only need you,
the best father in the world,
who will never leave you.

LOVER

Lover of my soul,
take complete control,
You take me higher,
than I can aspire,
or even conceive,
a constant perfect lover,
never willing to deceive.

Awesome Lover, Protector, and Confidant,
always blessing me with what I want,
how did I make it without you?
I just don't understand it,
Lover set me free,
awaken my senses to be just me.

Caresser, undresser of my innermost feelings,
that quiet time with you leaves me with healing,
healing I can't get from anyone else in the world,
bringing me to realize I'm your special girl.

Yes, we all have the choice to try and discover
having Jesus as the captain,
your one true lover.

RATHER LIFT JESUS!

Through trials and tribulations,
putting Satan under my feet,
because I am His creation,
from before I was in my mother's womb,
I was predestined and groomed
to be a vessel for Christ,
living, breathing the anointed life.

Rather lift Jesus!
Than break the vow,
the Savior has given me to show you how
to enjoy yourself to the fullest,
keep lifting Jesus, He'll see you through it
.

Whatever the situation
in your heart and soul,
if you rather lift Jesus, He will make you whole.

CELEBRATE YOUR SPIRIT

Look to the heavens
high above the stars,
celebrate your spirit
it makes you who, you are.

When things happen that are out of your control,
celebrate your spirit
inside of the soul.

Just think about the miracle inside you that can heal it,
your energy and style
makes you shine farther than a mile.

Spewing from your spirit
should be a continual praise and gratitude,
celebrate your spirit and positive attitude,
it can move mountains out of the way.

Celebrate your spirit.
your spirit, everyday!

HE SAVED ME

He saved me, so that I may live.
He saved me, to be a blessing and give,
He saved me, so I can stand up and be strong.
He saved me, to show other's where I belong.
He saved me, to inspire up lift and refire.
He saved me, to kingdom build for the Messiah.
He saved me, to be a soldier in the army of the Lord!
He saved me, to forget the past and go forward.
He saved me, without a second thought to it.
He saved me, because He knew I could do it.
He saved me, to alert everyone I can tell,
choose Christ as your personal Savior to escape from hell!
Be saved, He saved Me!

SMACKED DOWN

I am destined to be adorned with a crown,
a crown of jewels,
because as a Christian, I followed his rules.

The best humanly possible I could
we all fall short of the glory of God
and this is understood.

So when the Devil tries to entice you,
just smackem down!
Like your suppose to.

GRACE=

God's rewards and charity encourages!
God's rewards and compassion envelopes!
God's rewards and compassion encourages!

Grace
His grace, God's grace is sufficient and unrelented.
Grace in the place of life.
Grace in the space of life.
Grace in the race of life.

INHERITANCE ON YOUR LIFE!

Walk boldly!
Stake your claim.
Superior feelings.
No one to blame.
Inheritance on your life.
Free will Jesus gives.
Be an encourager.
Live and let live.

As far as the eye can see,
naked realism and truth
He displays daily to thee.
Unmasking the Devil and all evil spirits
granting supernatural blessings
you can fill it.

Be a walking, breathing, living testimony,
on the inheritance on your life.
You are a descendant of Abraham
who was a friend of God.

Blessing, anointing, fulfilling prophecy
could never be hard,
for the Creator Extraordinaire,
granting you favor everywhere.

From the mountain peaks
to the valley lows
supernatural blessings from Him just flows and flows.

Grab and claim the inheritance on your life
be a blessing to others and do what's right.

37

DESTRESSING

Confessing to the mind,
opening your life to Christ you'll find,
undressing within the heart,
living by faith is the way to start.

Regressing away from the past,
believing the Saviors love will last,
trusting spiritually the troubles will flee,
destressing the soul miraculously.

Bending, stretching, moving, twisting, reaching,
for that peaceful moment,
that's quietly spent,
longing, hoping, wishing, praying,
for what's heaven sent.

Destressing
leaving behind all cares,
watching the sun come up in the early morning air.

Destressing following your minds thoughts to a caressing
way,
take a little time to destress the day.

Enjoy the space, the area, the place,
where Christ takes you to destress the face.

The heart and the soul
relaxing you to make you whole,
whole in Him you will find,
destressing with Christ,
heals the mind.

BIND IT!

Grab it, hold it, push it, kick it, bind it
the enemy will try and devour (us)
because we are children of the God
who has infinite power.

Arise to your test
give it just a glance
it's a spiritual attack on your circumstance.

Bind it!
In the name of Jesus!
We can command demons to flee.
We are covered with renewed mercies daily.

Bind it!
Charge your assigned angels of mercy and protection
to place you in the right direction
to keep the Devil and all harm and danger away
wrap it up and toss it today.

Bind it!
our God is there with His shield and sword
waiting to awaken in you and be heard
ready to sleigh for you, listening for your word
to bind it !!!!

CONCLUSION

Come quickly swiftly to your own conclusion,
amidst the hustle and bustle and confusion.
Consider eternity with no pain
no hurts, or cares or stress
it's not an illusion.
moving, to your destresser,
with renewed love and grace to create a fusion.

Between the souls Jesus will reclaim!
If you fall down
jump up and try again.
Refuse to give in to the weapons of this world
don't let Satan give you delusions,
remember while the blood is warm in your veins to make
Christ like conclusions.

BOW BEFORE THE KING!

Kneel down, get down, lay down
bow before the King
lift up your voice
let your heart sing.

Praise to the one
who is my (our) everything
wake up! get up!
Don't stop moving.

Present (extend) yourself to the Lord
don't stop pursuing.

Bow before the King!
The Lord is the be all to end all
who will catch you when you fall.

Bringing back to remembrance
all that He has to offer
no reason for strife or to be a pauper.

Bow before the King
to show fervent homage
secure your salvation
be free from bondage.

TWINKLING

In a twinkling of an eye
you could be gone.

Leaving friends and family to go on
on without you.

What is your legacy,
are you all you thought you'd be?
Did you live outside the box,
or were you idle waiting to unlock?

The secret door of what life had in store,
well it's over now,
no longer can you complain.

The blood is no longer running warm in your veins,
did you take the twinkling moment before you left?

41

To settle up with God on all regrets,
or did you pretend as if you didn't know?

He sees all and will judge you so,
please be advised accepting Jesus as your personal Savior,
is the only prize.

Why!
Because He was crucified, suffered and died.

Who else do you know,
who could go through,
who loves beyond measure,
consistent and true?

No one but Christ will see you through,
in a twinkling of an eye,
you could be gone,
live for good and get carried home!

 ## OUR HANDS

Their hands, my hands, your hands, our hands
are they ready to extend?

Extend out to be kind
to be patient and gentle and ease someone's mind.

Who may quietly be going through their own painful story,
lend out your hands,
help them, bless them, from worry to glory.

Where are your hands?
What are they doing?
Through the stages of life, model your hands after the
Savior Christ.

Lend, bend your hands, move your hands,
to the Christian crusade,
your mark on the world,
will be your legacy
use your hands as they ought to be
to fulfill God's prophecy.

I HAVE A KING PARENT!

King of my vessel,
controller of my soul.
Worship is what I'll do,
praise will be my role.

From the quintessential moments,
when I took my first breath,
destined to be a Christian,
while learning my first steps.

Moving forward,
growing up, sought an excellent shepherd,
Pastor to help fill my cup.
The cup of wisdom, knowledge, and truth,
accepting Christ early coming from my youth.

Progressing through trying teenager years,

standing strong as a Believer,
through all my fears,
now as a woman,
molded, sculpted, and true,
He's giving me everything,
I promise you, I acknowledge Him in everything.

This is the reason my parent is King.
King to all!
So please won't you come,
experience love, joy, happiness, and fun?

Yes, I have a King parent,
it's not difficult to understand it,
Matthew 7 says ask and you shall receive,
whether it's silver or gold you can achieve,
all that life has to offer,
just ask your king parent whose known as the author.

Just ask your King parent!
Yes, He also belongs to you.
He's waiting with open arms to receive you.
This is true!
This is why, I love my King parent!

 ## I AM A TEMPLE

I am a temple,
we all are temples,
a walking, living temple,
body of Christ,

are you willing to be saved,
and commit to sacrifice,
to be free from being enslaved,
from the things of the world,
that rob us and makes us fear the grave,
to live as a temple is just,
to die is gain,
absence from the body,
is presence with Christ.

He's the temple in us all a beacon of light.

GOD'S INTENTION!

To have love in a society infected with evil,
to enlighten our hearts to be of help to all people,
to reach back , pull up, assist in the gain,
cherish the flowers , sun , and the rain,
that comes into all of your lives
on a daily basis.

We must have trials and tribulations,
to appreciate His final oasis,
an oasis of unique, infinite possibilities,
reflective of the glory from the Trinity!

UNFORTUNATELY

It's unfortunate to see
you don't acknowledge or care about me.

I woke you up this morning
with renewed mercy.

Idly by I waited, and sighed
wanting for you to realize,
I put the stride in your step,
the beat in your heart,
fought back all fiery darts
of the enemy who tried to destroy you endlessly.

Gave you breath of life,
to conquer all situations.
Give me my time,
not just when you have frustrations.

Worship me in high exaltation,
unfortunately,
I know you all to well,
devotion is expected of you,
as time will tell,
which path you choose to go will soon be unveiled.

CANT YOU SEE?

Cant you see?
God promises to meet you at your level of expectancy.

As far as the eye can see
have faith the size of a mustard seed.

Which in actuality
is really quite small.

Strong faith, unwavering faith, will fall a fresh upon thee
causes blessings to immerse on thee.

Wow!
Cant you see?

What's on the horizon
just open your eyes, then look towards the sky.

Then stretch your arms up and wide
let your anointing just glide
over your life, cant you see faith cancels strife!

PATH OF THE RIGHTEOUS

The path of the righteous gets brighter and brighter.
Never ceasing in prayer takes you higher and higher.
It engraves your name in the book of life.
Alleviating all misery and strife.

47

Stay on the path of the righteous.
Share, love, and give.
Most importantly live as you should live.
Adoring Christ through all of life's weather.

Creating that bond with Him that won't ever sever,

that will uphold through turbulent times,
the path of the righteous is the key, you will find.

DIVINES

Every knee shall bow!
Every tongue confess!
Without utterance or distress
Jesus Christ is our lord and personal Savior.

Here to save the world.
Touch a heart.
Anoint a spirit.

He's with us every second of the day,
be still and hear it.
Walking with us and to bless
removing strong holds that try and depress.

Allowing each individual to
bask in His divines,
Jesus Christ is the center of life,
we all need to find what inclines us.

Trust and believe it's His divines!

BEST WE CAN

We are destined as a people to be the best we can,
to be ordained with a crown in our heavenly land,
a crown of brilliant jewels,
because as Christians we followed His rules.

The best humanly we possibly could
going towards having eternal life.
Being good, now we all fall short of the glory of God,
but representing the King truly aint hard!

So when the Devil tries to entice you with foolishness,
saying he's your friend.
Look him square in the eye,
say on Christ is where I stand.

Then chuckle and grin
say "with Christ all things are possible."
You are cast down to your den
look to Jesus and say I trust you my friend.
Were just trying to do the best we can.

LIVING LIFE

Living life
a human sacrifice.

Giving honor to the master
who alleviates strife.

Standing strong
holding on.

Reaching for that unknown
unknown existence,
which will gratify the bareness in the soul,
that helps you maintain
the inner peace we all want to behold.

Unwinding the mind,
trying to find,
that common link that free's us,
cherish this thought it's Jesus.

FINALLY

Finally!
It has occurred to me
just merely living, isn't my destiny!
I deserve the best that life has to offer.
I'm a child of God.
He is my father.

He has outlined my prosperity and keys to life.
Promising me all I desire
if I accept Christ and claim my inheritance in Jesus name.

He will bring it to pass like the sun and the rain,
practicing dwelling in a Christian life.
Being righteous and true,
apologizing for strife.

God understands our finally before we do.
He's there with open arms to carry you through.

The captive soul can be free,
experiencing the goodness the Lord has for me,
in the land of the living.
reaping the harvest of my giving,
we serve a mighty God and I am grateful rest assured,
finally, we can see our vision no longer blurred!
Finally!

 ## COLORBOUND RIOTS

Riots within the mind
ancestry, history, legacy, generational lifeline.

Chase the dream, not the competition
define your existence.

Never conform!
Just design and align your dreams to the Creator's master
plan.

Achieve all endeavors, just stand and expand!

PASSIONS

Passions
like the morning dew,
that beads up and trickles down over you.

Inhibitions that won't prevent you,
from experiencing the life of ecstasy.

Tasting each moment slowly and freely,
explosions of intermingled minds,
the common link we all must find.

Trusting in spiritual choices and plans,
combining the souls of dreams and plans.

Satisfying that inner core,
the pressures are relieved, but you still crave more,
of that pleasure principle and what's in store,
that lingers everyday,
with a caressing voice of distinction to destress the day.

Hands of power to enter inside,
dictating exactly when it's time to ride,
in the passions we all hold on to,
waiting to experience what's meaningful and true,
follow your spiritual passions God will lead you.

Passions

FAITH

To have faith is to be sure of things we hope for
willing to leap over mountains and explore.
To be certain of the things we can't see
moving forward towards victory.
Astonished not of favor miraculously
it was by their faith
that people of ancient times won God's approval.
Willingness to trust and not be cruel,
by faith Abel offered a better sacrifice than Cain,
through faith healing comes just like in the rain.

It was faith that kept Enoch from dying.
Instead he was taken up to God
and nobody could find him.

No one can please God without faith.
Realizing God exists when there is no trace,

Faith

FOREIGNERS

Foreigners and refugees on earth
seeking spiritual validation and worth.

Heavenly country prepared by God
intricately developed origination from sod.

Here in foreign land to pass God's test
knowing His love and to give us His best.

Messiah far more than all treasures
kingdom jewels, crowns, and pleasures.

Foreign yet designed in His mind
matchless Lamb of God through all lifetimes.

 ## SHOULD I GO ON?

Should I go on?
There isn't enough time
to go back through generational life lines.

To speak of Gideon, Barak, Samson, Jephthah, David,
Samuel, the prophets
through unwavering faith they persevered, and fought it.
Yes! Whole countries and won
they did what was right
and received God's son.

They shut the mouths of lions
without even trying
just elevating their voices and testifying.

Put out fierce fires
calling on the messiah
increasing their beliefs to take them higher.

Escaped being killed by the sword
knowing in their minds it was the Lord.

Dead relatives raised back to life
should I go on
about the miracles of Christ!

MAKES A WAY

He makes a way
out of no way.
He makes cries turn to smiles
because He knows you're His child.

He makes a way when all hope is lost,
He anoints and blesses at any cost.
He makes a way when your sick and can't get well.
He makes a way for you to tell,
everyone about His mercy and grace,
He makes a way to slow down the pace.

He makes a way for you to know,
He's a doctor, lawyer, mother, lover, sister, brother, friend.
He makes a way to keep you standing.

THE NAMES OF THE LORD

Elohim: the Creator of heaven and earth.
The Master of validation and worth.

El-Shaddai: the God almighty of blessings,
the Originator of all that's manifesting.

Adonai: My Lord and Master
Perfect Prince of Peace.

Calmer of disaster.
Jehovah-Jireh: My Provider

the one who brings me through the fire.

Jehovah-Rapha: My Healer, Concealer.
Who makes tragedies sweet!
Jehovah-Nissi: My Victory, My Standard,
keeping me humble and balanced.

Jehovah-Shalom: My Peace, reminding me in prayer to
never cease.

 # COMPLETELY

Completely finished this poetic dream
breathed in my spirit from God's stream
choose Christ today and savor life,
living for the King
aiming to be just and right.

Travels throughout your mind and heart
completely trusting God is the part
we all must get to,
to eventually see the God of heaven supplying all your
needs
completely!!!!

AVAILABLE INSIDE

Available inside
to slide, to glide, to ride
on a mystical magical voyage.
Journey to the inner most part
available inside.
To soothe and relive the heart,
a heart that is aching
from the pressures and pains of the world.
To manifest and unfurl
available inside.

For you to run, to race, to escape with and to
that serene place
available inside of thee.
Sit, lay, bend, kneel down allow Christ to be
available inside thee.

FREE

As a man thinks in his heart so i⌐
Stop living the lie and ju⌐
Why not give God th⌐
He blessed you from your ⌐
He's ma⌐
Giving all Hi⌐
As turmoil
choos⌐

Take Christ's hand on ⌐
just be fre⌐

MUSTARD SEED

Faith of a mustard seed
it's all that's required,
to obtain what you need,
trust in God the higher being.

He's all knowing and seeing,
leap up towards your faith,
grab your super-natural gifts this day.
Understand a little faith goes a long way,
a living testimony here to say,
faith of a mustard seed,
which is so small,
will give the victory to all.

PEACE IN THE SANCTUARY OF MY MIND

Peace in the sanctuary of my mind.
thoughts of my friend and our lifetime.

Slowly, I rewind time that was spent
thanking the Lord for cherished moments.

Quietly, yet so softly
I say her earthly name Charard
peace and somberness
because she was a child of God's.

EVICTIONS

Eviction of the restrictions in your soul.
So long to suffering, pain and being out of control.
Say goodbye, farewell to addictions,
conflictions, restrictions, convictions.

Miscarriages, torn marriages,
discontent and baggage within.

Rejoice! In laying prostrate before God.
Lay it all out by surrendering all.
Passions, desires, dreams, lusts,
knowing in your heart there's only one you can trust!
Jesus !!!!!

FORGIVE AND LIVE

Forgive, why not?
Live, why not?
Be compassionate and give, why not?

We have the free will to choose.
Choose our battles.
Opening up our souls to forgive.
Move forward let the Devil know he has no control.

That you are going to love all your brethren.
Share the message of salvation.
Forgive, live, and keep caring with compassion.

YES, HE BLED!

From the fore skin of our toes
to the crown of our heads,

Jesus died for us.
Yes, He bled!

Immersed all around,
He hears every sound.

Encamped in armor to protect us!
Striking the burdens that attempt to test us.

He cast out wickedness
and negative talk that's said.

Jesus died for us.
Yes, He bled!

He's closer than a mother, sister, husband, wife, or brother.
Omnipotent is He, like no other.

He wants us to petition His throne,
to secure our eternal life,
when we go back home.

Jesus died for us.
Yes, He bled!

WHAT TIME IS IT?

It's time to move, run, walk, and roll.
Even though the world sometimes is cold.

It's time to gather soldiers.
And build a kingdom for Christ the Lord!

Don't be scared or filled with fear.
Jesus the Messiah is always near.

Reach, grasp, go quickly, and very fast.
Tell everyone you know
the time is now to prepare your soul.

What time is it?
It's time to dress in the armor suit of God.

Touching and agreeing just so He will hear it,
Hear your confessions of faith to Him.

Realizing your destiny is to eventually join Him.
To dance, shout, and give the angels help in praise,
to truly enjoy the glory days.

To order additional copies of:

A Tribute To
CHRIST
LaShawnda Allen-Ruffin

By Mail: **P.O. Box 528014**
Chicago, Illinois 60652-9998

By Email: **Shawn2news@ aol.com**

Retail price $14.95